AF381485

DEALING WITH ANXIETY ATTACKS

Simple ways of staying calm

Written by Maïlys Charlier
In collaboration with Céline Faidherbe
Translated by Emma Hanna

Health and Wellbeing 50MINUTES.com

Is avoiding situations that might trigger an anxiety attack a viable solution?

What is the best way to combat anxiety attacks?

Can anxiety be treated with medication?

DEALING WITH ANXIETY ATTACKS

SIMPLE WAYS TO STAY CALM

- **Problem:** anxiety attacks can arise unexpectedly, leaving their victim feeling paralysed. If they recur frequently, they can represent a serious problem.
- **Aims:** to reduce general anxiety levels and prevent anxiety attacks.
- **FAQs:**
  - How can I help someone who is having an anxiety attack?
  - Are stress and anxiety the same thing?
  - Can anxiety be cured?
  - How can anxiety affect our behaviour?
  - Is avoiding situations that might trigger an anxiety attack a viable solution?
  - What is the best way to combat anxiety attacks?
  - Can anxiety be treated with medication?

Anxiety should not be confused with stress, which usually stems from a specific source (an upcoming exam, a job interview, etc.), or temporary worries such as a minor illness. On the contrary, anxiety is a persistent, intense feeling of unease which may even feel like a physical weight lodged in your stomach or chest, and in extreme cases can cause anxiety attacks or panic attacks. It is generally defined as a generalised, irrational sense of fear. Anxiety attacks are a serious psychological ailment and can be treated in a number of different ways, depending on the individual in question and the severity of their condition.

People who suffer from anxiety experience irrational fear in the form of a general sense of unease. This condition affects between 4 and 7% of the population, but it is particularly difficult to diagnose due to the wide range of symptoms associated with it. In addition, certain symptoms of anxiety, such as stomach pains, breathing difficulties and attacks of tachycardia, can easily be mistaken for signs of a physical ailment. For this reason, in some cases it can take months or even years after the first symptoms appear for anxiety to be diagnosed correctly.

Anxiety attacks can prove life-ruining, as those who suffer from them often live in a permanent state of fear, constantly dreading the onset of another attack. Indeed, they often begin avoiding situations that could trigger an anxiety attack, and get trapped in a vicious circle wherein their attempts to avoid inducing a panic attack lead them to isolate themselves socially, which often causes them to fall into depression.

WHAT IS ANXIETY?

THE SYMPTOMS OF AN ANXIETY ATTACK

The first step in treating anxiety is to become aware of it, recognise the warning signs and identify the symptoms. It is also crucial to differentiate between stress, which is temporary, and anxiety, which is more permanent. While stress is generally caused by exceptional circumstances, anxiety is triggered by situations that we deal with on a regular basis. For this reason, it is important to be aware of the risk factors and situations which contribute to anxiety.

There are many different symptoms of anxiety, including heart palpitations, an accelerated heart rate, chest pains, breathing difficulties, hyperventilation, neck pains, headaches, dizziness, fainting spells, muscle tension, insomnia, restless sleep, nightmares, exhaustion, a dry mouth, the feeling of a heavy weight in your stomach or a lump in your throat, indigestion and reduced libido.

During an anxiety attack, it is also common to experience a sudden fear of one or more of the following circumstances: dying, impending doom, losing control of yourself, fainting, going mad and tragedy befalling close friends or family.

THE CAUSES OF ANXIETY

Anxiety can be caused by a number of different triggers, meaning that it can be difficult to identify the exact cause of a specific person's anxiety (especially as it may stem from more than one of these causes): a traumatic event (death, an accident, etc.), a genetic issue such as imbalanced neurotransmitters, depression, phobias, constant exposure to a stressful environment or being surrounded by other people who also suffer from anxiety. The catalysts for an anxiety attack can be biological, psychological, genetic or medical in nature, or it may stem from a kind of neurosis (internal conflict caused by forbidden desires or rejection).

Furthermore, the consumption of certain chemical substances (sodium lactate, nitrogen dioxide, etc.), stimulants (taurine, caffeine, etc.) or psychotropic drugs (cannabis, cocaine, etc.) can also contribute to the onset of an anxiety attack.

THE ROLE OF NEGATIVE THOUGHTS

Our brains can often fixate on negative thoughts for hours at a time, and this is undoubtedly another contributing factor to the development of anxiety. These thoughts are often intrusive and obsessive in nature, and have a symbiotic relationship with anxiety: high levels of anxiety make us more susceptible to negative thoughts, which in turn amplify our anxiety. It is therefore essential to break out of this vicious circle.

However, this can often be a difficult task, as anxiety tends to distort our perception of reality, and many sufferers' negative thoughts become uncontrollable as a result.

BASIC STEPS TO TAKE DURING AN ANXIETY ATTACK

If you feel an anxiety attack coming on, the first thing you should do is focus on your breathing. If the panic you are feeling is so severe that you cannot perform a breathing exercise, simply focus all your attention on each inhalation and exhalation. After focusing on your breathing in this way for several minutes, your body and mind should already feel calmer.

Next, it is important to avoid falling into a spiral of negative thoughts. If you have already suffered anxiety attacks on previous occasions, you will know that you are not going to die and that the attack will pass. Actively remind yourself that the attack will soon be over and that it is "only" anxiety. Try to focus on positive thoughts and reassure yourself that you are safe.

Become aware of your anxiety

It is essential to become aware of your anxiety, learn to recognise the signs of an impending anxiety attack (breathing difficulties, accelerated heart rate, hot flushes, cold sweats, stomach pains, chest pains, etc.), identify situations which tend to exacerbate your anxiety (phobias, fears linked to a traumatic memory, exhaustion, etc.) and pay close attention to your symptoms.

Identify the triggers

If your anxiety is so severe that it is causing frequent anxiety attacks, it is worth engaging in a period of self-examination in order to identify the factors that trigger these anxiety attacks and the root causes of your anxiety.

Talking to your close friends and family during this process can often provide you with invaluable insight, as they may be able to identify times when you are feeling anxious without even being aware of it. This will help you to put your finger on the common factors in the different situations that exacerbate your anxiety and identify its underlying causes.

PROFESSIONAL THERAPY

If you suffer from deep-rooted anxiety which stems from a traumatic experience, or if your anxiety is becoming unmanageable, there are many different types of therapy available which can help you combat both your anxiety and the underlying fears that fuel it.

In addition to classic psychoanalysis, you can also try alternative treatments such as cognitive behavioural therapy or short-term therapy such as Emotional Freedom Techniques (EFT) or Eye Movement Desensitisation and Reprocessing (EMDR). In any case, the most important thing is to find an approach that suits your individual needs.

One option is cognitive behavioural therapy, which can be an extremely effective short-term treatment for anxiety. The first step in this process involves observing and analysing the symptoms that the patient is suffering from, which then enables the psychotherapist to determine the negative thought patterns that are causing their anxiety. The next step is to start implementing various behavioural techniques which are chosen according to the type and severity of the patient's symptoms. The psychotherapist then helps the patient to gradually start facing the situations that scare them or trigger their anxiety attacks. If the therapy is successful, their symptoms will slowly diminish in severity and will eventually disappear completely.

Other types of short-term therapy have appeared more recently. Although the scientific rigour of these approaches has been called into question, they are relatively popular, which attests to their effectiveness.

EMDR is a technique which aims to use eye movement to help patients reprocess and become desensitised to the symptoms of post-traumatic stress. This method calls up the patient's traumatic memories while they move their eyes from side to side in the same way as in REM (Rapid Eye Movement) sleep. The aim of this treatment is to help make the trauma and anxiety associated with this memory easier to bear.

EFT is a technique which aims to make negative emotions such as fear, anxiety, stress, sadness and anger easier to manage. It was developed in 1993 by the American engineer Gary Craig (born in 1940), and involves the stimulation of various points on the body which are located on lines known as "energy meridians" in a manner similar to the Chinese practice of acupuncture. This method aims to expel negative energy from the body by tapping on these meridians.

TECHNIQUES FOR DEALING WITH ANXIETY ATTACKS

Although medication is the most effective short-term treatment for anxiety, there are also a variety of natural methods you can adopt to help you manage it. Anti-anxiety and anti-depressant drugs should only be taken after consulting a doctor, and most patients report that their symptoms resurface if they stop taking them.

Given that everyone's experience of anxiety is different and has different root causes depending on their life experiences, genes and various other factors, it is unsurprising that there are many different ways of dealing with anxiety. These include tried and tested techniques such as breathing exercises, meditation and exercise, as well as some less common treatments that may vary in effectiveness depending on the individual in question. It is up to you to experiment with these different approaches in order to find one that works for you and helps you to overcome your anxiety, whether as a short-term or long-term solution.

BREATHING EXERCISES

Breathing exercises are the most fundamental method of managing anxiety attacks. Indeed, breathing generally becomes more difficult in the throes of an anxiety attack, and can accelerate to such an extent that it causes a bout of coughing. Regaining control over your breathing also helps you to slow down your heart rate and gradually calm down your emotions.

Your immediate reaction to the onset of an anxiety attack should therefore be to focus all of your attention on your breathing. Concentrate on the feeling of air moving through your nose and throat, the way your stomach moves in and out, the feeling of your lungs filling up with air and the noise of each inhalation and exhalation.

The best way to prepare for a potential anxiety attack is to practise some breathing exercises, as this will make it easier for you to perform these exercises in the middle of an anxiety attack.

Start by practising abdominal breathing in order to master the basic technique before moving on to the more advanced exercises.

There are a number of different breathing techniques that you can adopt during a panic attack. These techniques can also be used to help you relax in normal circumstances.

- **Controlled breathing:** this technique involves counting to a certain number while you inhale, and then counting to the same number when you exhale. The most difficult aspect of this exercise is to keep your breathing regular. Ideally, you should try to count to six, although you can also count as high as nine if you feel comfortable doing so.
- **Abdominal breathing:** this is a simple breathing exercise which can reduce stress almost instantaneously. Like with classic conscious breathing exercises, the first step is to become aware of your breathing. Next, breathe in through your nose for a few seconds, letting your stomach expand, then contract your stomach as much as possible as you exhale. After five cycles of abdominal breathing you should perform five cycles of regular breathing, and so on.

- ***Ānāpānasati* (or "mindfulness of breathing"):** this breathing technique is used in a form of Indian meditation known as *vipassanā*, and involves pausing between each inhalation and exhalation, as well as focusing on each movement of your lungs.
- ***Prāṇāyāma* (or "breath control"):** this breathing exercise is associated with yoga, and can reduce anxiety within minutes. It involves a series of inhalations known as *pūrak*, exhalations known as *rechak*, and retention of breath known as *kumbhak*, which are alternated in a balanced manner in order to establish a rhythm.
- **Coherent breathing:** this breathing technique reduces stress and helps users to better control their heart rate. In practice, it involves inhaling and exhaling six times per minute (meaning that each inhalation and exhalation should last for five seconds) for a total time of five minutes. Each inhalation and exhalation should last for the same amount of time, and they should flow smoothly into each other without pauses between them. However, while focusing on your breathing in this way, you must also consciously relax each area of your

body, starting with your face and then moving on to your tongue, throat, hands, diaphragm and eventually your feet. This makes the exercise much more difficult.

MEDITATION AND MINDFULNESS

If you suffer from anxiety, meditation can help you to gain greater control over your emotions and, by extension, your anxiety, as well as helping to soothe the cycle of negative thoughts. Meditation allows you to "switch off" and take a step back from negative or intrusive thoughts, as well as reducing stress and anxiety and even helping you sleep better. Furthermore, meditation activates the left prefrontal cortex, which is associated with positive emotions.

According to studies carried out by Svea and Arist von Hehn, the authors of *La pleine conscience : Apprendre à méditer au quotidien !* ("Mindfulness: Learn to meditate on a daily basis!", 2015), meditation also improves our health, as it helps us to develop a closer relationship with our own body and handle physical and emotional pain more effectively, strengthens the immune system, reduces stress and better equips us to manage it.

Meditation can be coupled with mindfulness to make it even more effective. Mindfulness involves focusing your attention on the present moment and your senses, so mindfulness meditation simply means concentrating on the here and now while also examining your thoughts and emotions, letting them pass through your mind without trying to control or analyse them. Mindfulness meditation is therefore a way of reaching a state of complete mindfulness.

To practise mindfulness meditation, adopt the lotus position (cross your legs and rest your feet on your thighs, keeping your back and head as straight as possible, then rest your hands on your knees, which should be touching the floor) in a quiet room and focus on your breathing. Banish all thoughts about your worries and everyday problems, and let your thoughts flow freely until you are fully aware of your own breathing.

By practising regularly, it is also possible to apply active meditation. When you feel an anxiety attack coming on, engaging in active meditation can help you stay in control and prevent you from being overwhelmed by anxiety and the storm of negative thoughts it brings with it.

The premise of active meditation is simple: it simply involves meditating while carrying out everyday activities. In other words, it is the act of entering a state of mindfulness while also remaining fully focused on the task at hand. During an anxiety attack, engaging in active meditation can help you concentrate on your breathing and eventually calm down.

EXERCISE

Exercise is an excellent way of working off stress or anxiety while also improving your general health. Physical activity can help you release negative energy and unwind after a stressful day, and may also improve your sleep, which will in turn leave you less vulnerable to anxiety. Exercising also boosts serotonin and dopamine levels, which helps regulate your moods and can help to prevent depression.

HOMEOPATHY

Homeopathy can be defined as "a system of therapeutics [...] which was founded on the stated principle that 'like cures like,' *similia similibus curantur*, and which prescribed for patients drugs or other treatments that would produce in healthy persons symptoms of the diseases being treated" (Britannica). In other words, homeopathic treatments for a particular condition consist of minute doses of a substance that would, in a larger (meaning toxic) dose, cause that same condition in a healthy individual.

Of course, it can be difficult to identify a viable remedy for anxiety, given that it can be caused by a plethora of different factors and manifests very differently from one individual to the next. Nevertheless, a trained homeopath can prescribe a personalised remedy which takes your specific worries and behaviours into account – after all, homeopathy is a holistic approach which aims to treat each individual as a whole. As such, when a patient consults a homeopath regarding a specific ailment, the treatment will not just focus on that problem (as is the case with traditional medicine), but instead takes the patient's psychological wellbeing, lifestyle and medical history into account as well.

SOPHROLOGY

Sophrology is an approach to personal development which is based on the practices of a number of other disciplines, such as hypnosis, phenomenology, yoga, meditation and relaxation. It aims to help practitioners manage stress more effectively, boost their self-confidence and find inner harmony.

Sophrology exercises are all based on at least one of four key principles: listening to your body, stress management, self-confidence and life values. Practising sophrology can considerably boost the quality of life of someone who suffers from anxiety.

RELAXATION TECHNIQUES

As its name suggests, relaxation is a great way of soothing stress and anxiety. There are a number of different relaxation techniques that can help you to better manage stress and anxiety on a daily basis:

- **Progressive muscle relaxation:** this technique involves systematically contracting and relaxing one muscle after another, and can be used as a long-term strategy for managing anxiety. Progressive muscle relaxation should be practised while lying down with your body as relaxed as possible. Start by tensing your hand, then your forearm, and then relax your entire arm. Continue this process, gradually working your way upwards and tensing then relaxing each muscle on the way. Try using the following order: right arm, left arm, jaw, face, neck, shoulders, chest, pelvis, legs and feet. Whatever order you choose, the most important thing is to take your time over each muscle and make sure that every last drop of tension is drained from your body.

- **Relaxation breathing:** as its name suggests, this technique involves focusing on your breathing. Take several minutes to breathe calmly, inhaling slowly and deeply as you do so; this will have an immediate relaxing effect, and you will soon find yourself feeling much calmer.

- **Self-hypnosis:** this technique should be practiced while lying comfortably on the floor (feel free to cover yourself with a blanket if you are sensitive to the cold). Imagine that your body

is getting heavier and heavier, from the top of your head to the tips of your toes. You will soon enter a state of total relaxation.
- **Relaxation using music:** it is possible to relax simply by listening to music which has been specially developed for this purpose. Relaxing music, which can also be used as an aid when practising meditation, tends to consist of long pieces of music featuring slow, repetitive rhythms. This music is often instrumental and draws inspiration from classical, religious, minimalist and ambient music.

BACH FLOWER REMEDIES

Bach flower remedies are alcoholic solutions containing plant matter which were developed by Dr Edward Bach (British doctor, 1886-1936) in the early 20th century. They can be purchased in certain pharmacies and organic stores, and can be combined to create a solution adapted to your needs.

- The Rescue Remedy is recommended for those who suffer from phobias and who require instant treatment for anxiety attacks. This solution was invented by Dr Bach and combines a number of the other flower remedies (Star of Bethlehem, Rock Rose, Clematis, Impatiens and Cherry Plum). It is often specifically recommended for those who have a fear of flying, but it can be used to combat any type of anxiety attack.

- Many Bach flower remedies are reportedly useful for the treatment of anxiety, including Chicory, Rock Rose, Aspen, Star of Bethlehem and Sweet Chestnut.
- Red Chestnut is recommended for those who specifically fear that tragedy will befall their loved ones.
- The following Bach flower remedies can be used to combat general fears: Aspen, Crab Apple, Rock Rose, Sweet Chestnut.
- Aspen and Heather are recommended for those who experience recurring irrational fears.
- The following Bach flower remedies can be used to combat everyday stress: Impatiens, Vervain, Vine and Water Violet.

YOGA

There are many different styles of yoga, but they are all based on the same fundamental principles, which include meditation, breathing exercises and mindfulness. Practising yoga on a regular basis generally involves these exercises, as well as aspects of tai-chi (a Chinese martial art), Pilates or Qigong (a Chinese system of postures and movement designed to promote the flow of energy).

Practising yoga aids physical and mental relaxation and can boost your wellbeing. By focusing your attention on the movement of your own body, yoga can help you avoid thought patterns that lead to anxiety; indeed, it is impossible to practise yoga without mindful concentration, which is the key to allowing your body, mind and nervous system to relax. The breathing exercises involved also help with this relaxation process.

Yoga is most effective and most likely to be helpful in the long term when it is practised on a regular basis, meaning at least once a week.

AUTOGENIC TRAINING

Autogenic training is a relaxation technique that was developed by the German doctor Johannes Heinrich Schultz (1884-1970) in the early 20th century, and can help reduce stress and anxiety.

This method consists of five phases: weight, heat, heartbeat, abdomen, breathing and heart. It is recommended to master each phase before moving on to the next; as such, you should spend a week focusing on the sensation of weight before moving on to heat-based exercises. Each phase of this technique should be practised while lying down with your arms by your sides, legs close together, feet turned outwards and hands lying flat on the floor.

- **Weight.** This phase involves visualising each muscle as you relax it, all while focusing on the feeling of weight and heaviness in that part of your body.
- **Heat.** Imagine heat spreading gradually through your entire body from head to toe.
- **Abdomen.** Focus on your internal organs: your stomach, intestines, lungs, etc. Try to feel the heat of these organs and relax each of them in turn.
- **Heart.** Concentrate on your heartbeat without trying to control it.
- **Breathing.** Focus on your breathing until it is slow and relaxed.

Once you have mastered each of these phases, you are ready for a session in which each of these stages flows into the next, leaving you in a state of intense relaxation.

MUSIC

It is a well-known fact that music can have a calming effect, but listening to music in order to relax and calm your anxiety is not a universally effective technique. However, if it works for you, taking some time to listen to songs or artists that make you feel good can be a powerful way of helping you relax and think about something other than your anxieties. Choose your music carefully, as it will affect your emotions: for example, listening to classical music is more relaxing than listening to heavy metal.

One exercise you can try while listening to music is to attempt to pick out each of the different instruments being played: focus on the sound of the guitar, the beat of the drums and the bass in turn, trying to totally separate it from the rest of the song. This will give you something to concentrate on, and will therefore distract you from your anxieties.

OTHER TIPS AND TRICKS

Calming food

Substances contained in certain foods can help to combat everyday stress. These substances include fibre (found in red beans, peanuts, lentils, raspberries, etc.), slow-release carbohydrates (found in wholegrain bread, oatmeal, sweet potatoes, etc.) and omega-3 (found in oily fish). More specifically, the following foods also have beneficial properties:

- almonds are rich in iron, zinc and fatty acids and help combat mental exhaustion, meaning that they can prevent low energy and increased anxiety;
- blueberries have many beneficial properties and are rich in antioxidants, which help combat anxiety;
- taking a cup of camomile tea or a valerian tablet in the evening before going to bed can have a soothing effect that encourages restful sleep.

Food supplements

There are many food supplements which can help combat anxiety.

- Magnesium helps combat stress, meaning that magnesium deficiency can make it more difficult to overcome anxiety. Taking a course of magnesium supplements for 20 to 30 days should be enough to remedy this imbalance.
- Omega-3 fatty acids are also an effective means of fighting anxiety. The recommended daily allowance is 500 mg, which is the equivalent of two meals containing oily fish per week. Omega-3 can also be found in certain vegetable oils such as rapeseed, soy or walnut oil, as well as in nuts, linseed, watercress, cabbage and spinach.
- Gamma-Aminobutyric acid, also known as GABA, is an important neurotransmitter which helps regulate stress levels. As such, GABA deficiencies can lead to increased anxiety. This substance can be found in many foods, including broccoli, nuts, citrus fruits and bananas. The recommended daily allowance is 3 g for adults.

Avoid stimulants

If you suffer from anxiety, it is best to avoid stimulants such as alcohol, energy drinks, coffee and tobacco. Nicotine, caffeine and taurine actually increase the heartbeat and stimulate the nervous system, which could exacerbate a potential anxiety attack.

Think positive

There is nothing quite as calming as a bit of positive thinking! Focus on things that make you happy and calm you down, and banish the negative thoughts that are dragging you into a downward spiral.

Maintain a healthy sleeping pattern

Anxiety is very tiring, and anxiety attacks tend to become more frequent if you are not sleeping enough. To avoid getting trapped in this vicious circle, it is important to make sure that you are getting enough sleep – if necessary, start taking naps!

FAQS

HOW CAN I HELP SOMEONE WHO IS HAVING AN ANXIETY ATTACK?

If you are with someone who is having an anxiety attack, the most important thing is to remain calm so that you do not create an additional source of stress for them. If you are in a crowded or confined space, try to create some extra space around them or take them somewhere they will have more breathing room. Next, try to reassure them that they are in a safe environment and are safe with you. Help them to concentrate on their breathing, which will enable them to calm down quickly and allow the anxiety attack to pass.

ARE STRESS AND ANXIETY THE SAME THING?

There are subtle differences between stress and anxiety: stress tends to be a side effect of specific events (marriage, an exam, a job interview, pregnancy, etc.) and does not necessarily cause anxiety or anxiety attacks, although it can certainly be a contributing factor. On the other hand, anxiety is a more insidious problem which rarely has a single, easily identifiable cause. It tends to manifest as a constant presence within the sufferer's psyche, and often goes unnoticed both by the sufferer and by the people around them.

CAN ANXIETY BE CURED?

Although anxiety is not a condition that can be cured *per se*, it is certainly possible to treat it. Treatment will enable the sufferer to control their anxiety and avoid future anxiety attacks, even in times of stress or distress. Furthermore, techniques that alleviate everyday anxiety can also be applied during a future anxiety attack, allowing the sufferer to regain control more quickly and easily.

HOW CAN ANXIETY AFFECT OUR BEHAVIOUR?

Anxiety does not just affect our health and sleep, but also our behaviour and personality. A person who suffers from anxiety can develop psychological complexes, paranoia and phobias. As a result, their anxiety can drive them to adopt different behaviours, and they may become aggressive, irritable or hyperactive.

IS AVOIDING SITUATIONS THAT MIGHT TRIGGER AN ANXIETY ATTACK A VIABLE SOLUTION?

After suffering an anxiety attack for the first time, most people's first instinct is to start avoiding situations like the one that triggered the attack; as a result, many people who suffer from anxiety have self-isolating tendencies. However, this should never be used as more than a stopgap solution, because avoiding any kind of situation that could possibly trigger an anxiety attack is a slippery slope that can lead to a harmful pattern of avoidant behaviour which will prevent you living your life to the full.

WHAT IS THE BEST WAY TO COMBAT ANXIETY ATTACKS?

Given that the causes of anxiety differ from one person to the next, it is impossible to identify a single "miracle cure" that will work for everyone. Each treatment should be adapted to the patient's specific needs, taking their life experience and the causes of their anxiety attacks into account. In the end, it is up to each individual to find solutions that work for them. However, it is worth noting that breathing exercises and relaxation techniques are among the most effective methods of controlling anxiety.

CAN ANXIETY BE TREATED WITH MEDICATION?

Generally speaking, anti-anxiety and anti-depressant medication (which should never be taken without consulting a doctor) only tackles the symptoms of anxiety, not the root causes, and these symptoms will immediately return if you stop taking this medication.

We want to hear from you!
Leave a comment on your online library
and share your favourite books on social media!

FURTHER READING

BIBLIOGRAPHY

- Chapelle, C. (2016) *Le petit livre de la sophrologie.* Paris: Editions First.

- (2017) Crise d'angoisse : comment s'en sortir ? *Stress-solution.fr.* [Online]. [Accessed 25 July 2018]. Available from: <http://stress-solution.fr/crises-dangoisse-comment-sen-sortir>

- Ferris, P. (2013) *Le guide des fleurs du Dr Bach.* Paris: Marabout.

- (No date) Homeopathy. *Britannica.* [Online]. [Accessed 25 July 2018]. Available from: <https://www.britannica.com/science/homeopathy>

- Oswald, P. (2013) *Comprendre et traiter les troubles anxieux.* Brussels: ViVio.

- Oswald, P. (No date) Le trouble d'anxiété généralisée. *Medipedia.be.* [Online]. [Accessed 25 September 2017]. Available from: <https://fr.medipedia.be/troubles-anxieux/formes/le-trouble-anxicte-generalisee>

- Oswald, P. (No date) Troubles anxieux. *Medipedia.be.* [Online]. [Accessed 16 November 2017]. Available from: <https://fr.medipedia.be/troubles-anxieux/traitements/autres-therapies>

- Sayous, D.-J. (2014) *L'homéopathie. Tous les remèdes pour guérir en douceur les maux du quotidien*. Paris: Eyrolles.

- Schneider, C. (2017) Cinq techniques pour apprivoiser ses angoisses. *Marieclaire.fr*. [Online]. [Accessed 25 July 2018]. Available from: <https://www.marieclaire.fr/,5-techniques-pour-apprivoiser-ses-angoisses,20254,21360.asp>

- Von Hehn, S. and Von Hehn, A. (2015) *La pleine conscience : Apprendre à méditer au quotidien !* Paris: Ecolibris.

ADDITIONAL SOURCES

- Charlier, M. (2018) *Mindfulness*. Trans. Neal, R. Brussels: Plurilingua Publishing.

- Lemmens, A. (2018) *Yoga for Beginners*. Trans. Hanna, E. Brussels: Plurilingua Publishing.

- Radomme, B. (2017) *Overcoming Anxiety*. Trans. Neal, R. Brussels: Plurilingua Publishing.